Solace with or without you.

Ankita Tomar

BookLeaf
Publishing

India | USA | UK

Presentation by *BookLeaf Publishing*

Web: www.bookleafpub.com

E-mail: info@bookleafpub.com

ISBN: 9789360949327

First edition 2024

ACKNOWLEDGEMENT

I would love to hereby acknowledge the presence of all the loved ones during different phases of my life and to bless me with their experiences and to share the space alongside them. These unique and special experiences have made me what I am today, with all the learnings I had on human level, in terms of relationships I have with my family, friends and love interests.

My heartfelt gratitude to the holy god and his blessings, to sun, moon and all the celestial bodies who all are pretty significant to me and my journey so far.

Last but not the least, I am thankful for my family and friends for instilling the sense of calm, kindness and compassion in me. I am grateful for all the love, losses, learnings and blessings so far.

I am and will always be thankful for all the readers who took out their valuable time and decided to share it with me. All my love and blessings to you all. Here's hoping my verses can help you too find solace in your respective phases of lives. And, in the end it's when you love yourself, you tend to get closer to solace.

Coz, I am this pearl in my own solace, getting prepared for some great purpose.

Thank you! :))

No turning back.

It started with a pen
You asked for it.
I ended up giving my heart too.
Yeah, crazy me.

We danced like aliens in that party
Found our own comfort level.
Went on a tour together
Thankfully, I took my lead.

Back home, we felt uneasiness
Of not being together.
Found peace in each others music.
Okay, life was at it's best.

Disasters happen at the most unexpected time.
Isn't it?
And, this was it,
Your cameo role in my life was done.

At least I thought so.
And then, on one fine night
At 8 o'clock
Your mere apostrophe was enough to lure me
back.

I was at cloud nine.
The eagerness with which I get up and get to the college,
Surprisingly, all seems worthwhile.

We cleared all the bumps that came in way
And they lead us closer everytime.
Little did we know,
We're headed towards a dead end with no turning back.

You're the exclamation!

You're my cream of the cake.
You're that extra but adequate amount of tinge
of spice that suits me.
You're the rain that makes me full of soothing
scents by falling over me.
You're cup of tea in winters, warm and yum.
You're that glass of chilled water in deserts,
feels like heaven.
You're that melted yolk of half fry.
You're the air and the bread, giving purpose to
my life.
You're the cheer of joy, high-fiving the
confidence every now and then.
You're the windows to a beautiful view,
refreshing the vibes.
You're my favourite person.

You make time fly.

Your hard to resist sweetness, probably end up in
me being a diabetic.
Your top-notch humour, oh, I am a fan.
Your gentle care, it's so love.
Your every text, filled with emotions.
Your never ending talks, how desperately I want
them to keep going.
You make time fly, I guess I've stopped looking
at it now
Your specific observations, makes me blush
Your open heartedness, really appreciate that.
Your fan following, increasing day by day.
Your crazy games, love them all.
Your wierdness, my favourite.
You give reasons to smile every moment.
Just want to know,
Why am I this special to you?

Yearning for love.

The writer in me is shut,
The heart is all numb,
As if I don't feel anything, anymore.
No pain, no happiness,
Don't even bother to mention peace.

Every second, every moment,
I feel you around.
In someone else's eyes, in someone else's voice,
Or through references.
You're right there on my mind.

The mere thought of being with someone else,
It's terrifying to me.
For I don't wanna end up like this again,
As I don't have that courage,
I told you, I'll be shattered,
And now just have a look.

I am yearning for love in any form, be it just
friendships.
This weirdness is killing me.
I used to be someone else.
And I used to love that someone.

Last breath of our Love.

And, it all fell down,
Like a tower of cards.
Shattering the hopes,
Came the denial.
That was the last breath,
Our love has taken.
What if,
The courage is gone?
The rage is gone?
The mere trace of you,
Along with you, is gone.
Sleepless nights are all that I see,
Just if setting free really meant the same,
Smiling layer above those of pain,
The diamonds of tears try their very hard to
move past the brim,
Every time, I hold them,
Right there.
Coz, they're the only one I have with me here.

Asking for help.

You know this hour and keyboard have
something in common,
"Flow",
As one makes the emotions to flow,
And other makes fingers to glide in response to
that flow.

Scoffing it all for the whole day,
Not letting a single person know that I cry on a
daily basis,
I don't know if that's being brave or being
coward,
I accepted the fact that I have come a long way,
But there's something I am still not done with,
Something that's not letting me be in peace.

I look for ways, I look for days,
Nights hunt me down,
With only this pain that stays.

Swallowing me down,
Taking my shine,
Every single night,
With this darkness around,
Leaving me with this inner sound,

Which screams within me,
Asking for help.

Celestial bodies and you.

There's something similar in those celestial
bodies and you,
Maybe that's the reason why I wanna keep
looking,
Keep yearning for the closeness,
Keep desiring to touch,
And neither of you is stable.

So, my love!
Be the setting sun to surprise me with some
unique combination of colour everyday.

Be the moon, crescent or full, for just being
there.
And if not the moon, be that feel of inexistence,
longing to get back to existence.

Similarities and Control

That same accent,
Same love for sleep,
Same panicking about every dumb thing,
Same noticing everything,
Same concern,
Same expressions,
Same cuteness or maybe more.

Damn, why lord why?
Why are you testing my control.
You know it's really so hard.
I am already missing him a lot,
And seeing him in this lovely person, I find this
idiot more sweet.

Shooting Star.

The way you look at me,
It feels like a moment of serendipity.
All those cute efforts you make to win my heart,
Trust me! I melt just like an ice-cream in
summers.

That deliberate eye contact of more than a
minute,
woke butterflies in my stomach.
Guess what, my heart wants to flirt like so bad,
But I just can't.

Your smile, laughter and cuteness urges me to
hug you,
Whenever I see your lips at my eye level, I feel
like kissing,
I saw that calm that I guess I have power to
bring in your chaotic mind,
Really love how stupid faces you make,
Those two moles want me to bite them,
But I just can't.

As you tend to keep me at a safe distance,
And here I am falling for you at the pace of a
shooting star.

Wondering if wonders are real.

I wonder,
If you too have walked that path I had been to,
If you too have penned your feelings down with
my name on it,
If you too have thought about me and smiled,
If you too have created scenarios in your mind
about us,
If you too have missed me the way I do,
If you too have said it all to me on one fine day,
If you too have thought of regretting the same
the next moment,
If you too want to relive our moments together,
If you too feel it incomplete without me,
If you too are scared of losing me,
If you too have been wondering all these about
me,
If you too watch relatable stories to get a better
perspective,
Wondering if wonders are real cause if they are,
I would have had the answers by now.

Storm you brought along.

In came a storm, buried everything in snow,
Including the heart,
It started like a lovely cozy weather of winters,
Where it's been sunny during days and
extremely cold in the night.
Thanks to the blanket of love we had, but then,
One avalanche, blanket was gone and so were
you, and yet,
There are still scars of the storm you brought
along.

Nowhere in the vision.

Strawberries were sour,
Rose petals were heavy,
Music had no meaning,
Coz I had you completing me.
Loving me.
Well, everything got it's essence back
Except me,
I am drowning now,
Asking for a float to survive,
And you're nowhere in the vision.

I hate your cuteness.

You came in like a dream,
Full of love, emotions, passion.
Some cute flaws too.
Oh, I hated your made-up stories,
I hated our differences,
I hated when you messed with me,
Or maybe not.

Coz now that I am awake,
Why do I miss you, your stupidities,
And you, the dream?

Oh, I so wished it to keep going,
But you gotta wake-up sometime,
To face the reality,
And it shattered, the whole dream,
Gone in seconds.

Left some flashbacks, some meanings,
Or maybe a puzzle to solve,
If reasonably put together,
Can turn into a breakthrough.

The mistake!

As it came flying to me,
I hugged it with wide arms,
Just because it consisted you.

The you,
Whom I admired,
Whom I love,
Whom I can never forget,
Who just tug onto my heartstrings.

It came out to be the best blessing,
For the first few months,
And faded in last two,
The same way water evaporates in presence of
sunlight,
Leaving its mark over the ground.

Oh yes! It hurts!
A whole lot.
At least you would've given a hell good reason
to do so,
And it would be better accepted.
Coz the wound is green,
And I wish it to be green always.
So that I won't repeat it,
The mistake!

After this while.

I still have that thing for you,
Still miss that smile on my face,
Still waiting for some cues,
Still want my heart to skip a beat or two,
Still feel those thrills down my spine,
Still visualise a parallel universe that had us,
Still wish for it to be true,
Still daydreaming about it all,
Still struggling to find ways to keep you out of
my mind,

Even after this long?
Especially after this while.

Your ring.

I finally took it off
The ring
Which didn't fit me at all
Yet I was trying to mould it on my finger
And when it actually fit me in the end
It started scarring and hurting me
My face, especially.

I know it was pretty obvious
It doesn't fit me
I knew this since the beginning
But
Somewhere deep down
I knew I can work with it,
That it's okay,
"You don't get all served"

I tried, trust me I did
A whole lot
But it was just me trying
This imbalance took me
And inturn took what we had.

But you know
I always kept stretching

Kept giving chances
Kept things alive
Till the very end.

And now when I look back at my heart
I see a soldier fighting for his motherland,
All scarred, bruised and armed
In the camouflage,
Until his last breath for you.

I battled with my own self
Between my self respect and love
But
You know what stabbed me in the end
The ignorance.

You and the white colour.

You came in as white colour,
All plain and simple,
Yet classic.
One day,
You were the rainbow,
With both rain and sun,
For that moment,
You made me fall for you.
And then you faded in clouds,
Left me longing for the same weather.
After sometime,
You arrived unexpectedly,
This time more prominent,
I thought this time it'd be forever,
But it was just a bit longer.
Turns out,
You're back to white for me,
White with all the colours,
Yet colourless.

The pearl, its shell and the ocean.

I am this pearl,
Found in the ocean called home,
Being protected by this shell, my family.

The shell has this man,
Serving for the nation and embracing the
camouflage,
Man with heart of stone,
Who doesn't demand anything,
Though he wishes a lot,
But prefers to put that lid on the pot.

Then comes the most beautiful woman on earth,
The warrior who carried me inside for nine
months,
Fighting against all odds, grew me up a good
person,
Taught me values and ethics,
A perfect paradigm of sacrifice,
She questions a lot,
And her favourite one is,
You ate something or not?

And there's this idol of mine,

Played with him, fought with him,
And most importantly love and respect him a lot,
Be it the sound of airplane or monkeys that
frightened me,
He has always been the shade over my head,
The jam to the bread.

I, the pearl would've been lost,
If it weren't for these layers of shell and the
ocean,
The shine I reflect, delicacy I hold within,
And the strength I bear,
Correlates to their eternal love and care.

Struggles? Keep cruising.

Cruising.
We take overbridges.
We go for the crowd.
We slow down for wetness.
And hover it when dry.
Seems amazing?
Yeah.
Except.
It's instantaneous.
A limit that tends to zero.
Either no-where or now-here!
Former we profoundly refuse to believe.
Latter is how we keep going.
No matter what.
You know why?
Coz, limitations aren't enough.
They can never be.

Turning Pages.

Aging is like turning pages,
With the blow of life hitting hard,
Changing the plot, narrating a shot,
Transitioning it upside down,
The whole story.

Rush is taking over,
Time is controlling you, driven by hours,
You strive through.
Caressingly, the hands will be there,
Of your loved ones,
Keeping you sane within this madness.

Blessed are those who have them,
Blessed are those who keep them close,
Safe and warm, in their hearts.

Era of greatness.

Just like a baby he took time to process what's
going on.
He re-ate some meals, even skipped a few
thinking he already had.
That confused look he had when he was trying
to nod at being familiar to me.
All of it made me shiver, and why won't it, after
all, it's his blood in my veins.

I may not have been physically there all the time
for him,
But emotionally, I have felt every laughter and
every sigh of his.
Only I know how badly I wish him to get better.
Oh I wished it that day when I last visited him.
I wished it that day too when I last had a glance
on a video call.

I remember even during his sufferings he was
well aware of me.
Just if I could stand against the law of nature,
I would've wished for him to never take his
blessing hand away from us.
To never leave.

Here's a cruel saying,
"For everything that has ever started comes to an end."
And it was the end of an ERA!
An era of greatness.